THE SILENT SPACE WITHIN

Transforming Emptiness into Strength

ISHU RAJ

The Silent Space Within: Transforming
Emptiness into Strength

2025 Edition

ISBN-13 979-8896992271 [Paperback]
ISBN-13 979-8896992288 [Hardcover]

Publisher: Notion Press Media Pvt Ltd.
#7, Red Cross Road,Egmore,
Chennai, Tamil Nadu 600008

Dedication:

To everyone who has ever felt lost, you are not
alone.

CONTENTS

Part I:Embracing the Silent Space

Part II: Exploring the Space Within

Part III: Transforming Emptiness into Strength

Part IV: The Journey to Inner Strength

MISCELLANEOUS

Foreword

By the Author

In today's fast-moving world, where we are constantly
chasing success and distractions, there are moments when
we feel an unsettling emptiness within. It's a hollow
feeling, one that makes us question everything—*Who am
I? Why do I feel this way? What is my purpose?*

I've been there. For years, I struggled with that same
emptiness, trying to escape it through distractions,
achievements, and temporary happiness. But the more I
tried to fill the void, the deeper it seemed to grow. It
wasn't until I stopped running from it and started
understanding it that I discovered a powerful truth:
emptiness is not the end of the road. It can be a new
beginning—a space where healing and transformation can
happen.

*The Silent Space Within: Transforming Emptiness into
Strength* is the result of my journey. This book is written
for anyone who has felt lost, hollow, or disconnected. It is
not just a guide but a companion to help you understand
that emptiness is not something to fear. Instead, it can be a
space where we reconnect with ourselves, rediscover our
purpose, and find strength we didn't know we had.

Through these chapters, we will explore the reasons behind emptiness, its impact, and, most importantly, how to turn it into a source of growth and resilience. The lessons I've learned, the practical tools I've used, and the stories I'll share are meant to give you clarity, comfort, and hope.

I want you to know that you are not alone. Feeling empty doesn't mean you're broken; it simply means you are searching for something deeper. This search is a part of being human, and it is through this journey that we truly grow.

As you read, remember that the void you feel is not your enemy. It is a teacher, a guide, and a space waiting to be filled with purpose, strength, and light. Let this book help you embrace the silence within and transform it into a source of empowerment.

Welcome to this journey of healing and self-discovery.

With hope and sincerity,

Ishu Raj
Author of "The Silent Space Within"

Introduction

The Silent Space Within

Defining Emptiness and Its Universal Nature

Have you ever felt a void inside you, a hollow space that no achievement, relationship, or distraction could fill? This feeling—emptiness—is deeply unsettling yet profoundly universal. It's a quiet ache that leaves us questioning everything: *Why do I feel this way? What's missing? What's wrong with me?*

Emptiness isn't always sadness, loneliness, or fear, though it often disguises itself as those emotions. It's deeper and harder to define, like standing in a crowded room and still feeling utterly alone or achieving a long-sought goal and realizing it didn't bring the joy you expected.

The truth is, everyone experiences emptiness at some point. It may come from losing someone we love, failing at something we worked hard for, or feeling disconnected from ourselves and the world around us. For some, it comes in waves that pass quickly. For others, it lingers, growing quietly in the background.

What makes emptiness so challenging is its silence. It doesn't scream for attention the way physical pain does, but it has a profound impact on our thoughts, emotions, and decisions. It can make us question our worth, lose sight of our purpose, and even distance us from the people we care about.

But here's something I've learned: emptiness is not a sign of weakness or failure. It's a natural part of being human. And while it may feel overwhelming, it also holds incredible potential for growth and transformation.

My Motivation for Writing This Book

I didn't just learn about emptiness from books or observations—I've lived it. My journey through emptiness was one of the hardest chapters of my life. I faced countless backlashes, harsh criticism, and failures that left me questioning my abilities. Friends I thought I could rely on drifted away, and I found myself feeling neglected and alone.

There were nights when I cried in silence, too afraid to share my struggles. As an introvert, I felt trapped inside my mind, unable to express what I was going through. Depression crept in, whispering lies that I wasn't enough, that no one cared.

I can't tell you that it was easy or quick to overcome. But one day, I realized I had a choice: to let emptiness define me or to face it head-on. Slowly, I began to explore the feelings I had avoided for so long. I allowed myself to sit with the silence instead of running from it.

Through this process, I discovered small moments of joy I had overlooked before—the beauty of a quiet morning, the laughter of a stranger, the warmth of sunlight. I stopped searching for happiness in big accomplishments and learned to appreciate the little things that made life meaningful.

This journey helped me overcome the fears that had kept me from living authentically. I let go of the constant need to seek approval, stopped chasing perfection, and started celebrating my progress, no matter how small.

Writing this book is my way of sharing that journey with you. I know how lonely emptiness can feel, but I want you to know that you're not alone. I wrote this book to offer you comfort, guidance, and hope. If I could find my way through the darkness, so can you.

Emptiness as an Opportunity for Growth

For years, I thought emptiness was my enemy—a void I needed to escape. But I've come to realize that emptiness isn't something to fear. It's a space, a silent space, waiting to be filled.

When we experience emptiness, it's often because something in our life is out of alignment. The void forces us to pause, reflect, and ask ourselves hard questions: *What truly matters to me? What do I need to let go of? What do I want to create in my life?*

This isn't an easy process, but it's a necessary one. Emptiness can be a doorway to transformation. It strips away what no longer serves us and creates space for growth, healing, and self-discovery.

In my own life, emptiness taught me to let go of toxic relationships, unrealistic expectations, and the constant pressure to prove myself. It taught me to slow down and listen to my own heart. Most importantly, it showed me that I am stronger than I ever realized.

This book is about helping you see emptiness in a new light. It's not just about surviving the void; it's about embracing it as an opportunity for growth. Together, we'll explore why emptiness happens, how it affects us, and, most importantly, how we can transform it into strength.

You'll find practical tools, inspiring stories, and actionable steps to help you navigate your own journey. You'll learn that the silent space within you is not a place of despair— it's a place of potential, waiting to be discovered.

As you begin this journey, I want you to know that you are not alone. The feelings you carry are valid, and the struggles you face do not define you. Emptiness is not the end of your story—it's the beginning of something beautiful.

Let this book be a reminder: the silent space within you is not empty—it's full of potential.

PART 1

Making Sense of the Emptiness

*"Emptiness isn't something to fear, it's a space waiting to
be understood. In the quiet of the hollow, we begin to find
the truth of who we are."*

CHAPTER 1

What is This Empty Feeling?

"Why do I feel this way? Like there's something missing?"

You've probably asked yourself that question more times than you care to admit. Whether it's after a challenging experience, a period of emotional stress, or even during a random moment of quiet, that feeling of emptiness seems to creep up unexpectedly. So, what exactly is this "empty feeling"?

Let's break it down and understand what it really means, and more importantly, why it's okay to feel this way.

What Exactly is Emptiness?

At its core, emptiness is a sense of lack—a gap in our emotional, mental, or spiritual life. It's like there's something missing, but you can't quite pinpoint what it is. You might feel detached, as if you're not fully engaging with life around you. It could be a quiet ache in your chest, a mental fog, or a general sense of disconnection.

- *Emptiness is a temporary feeling that arises from internal or external factors.*

- *It can show up as a result of major life changes or from daily stress.*
- *It doesn't mean you're broken; it's a signal asking you to pay attention to your inner world.*

Emptiness isn't something to be afraid of. It doesn't mean you're broken or that something's wrong with you. In fact, it's a natural feeling that many people experience at different times. It's just a sign that something needs attention, whether it's your emotional well-being, your purpose, or your connections with others.

Emotional Emptiness: The Heart's Heavy Silence

This is the emptiness that most people experience in a deeply personal way. It's when you feel emotionally drained, as though your heart is just not fully in things anymore. Sometimes, it's the result of loss, a breakup, or just a difficult time in life. But it doesn't always have to be tied to a major event.

- *Emotional emptiness often shows up when we feel disconnected or unable to relate to others.*

- *It can make you feel like you're going through the motions of life, but without the depth or passion that once accompanied it.*

- *This type of emptiness can be especially hard because it feels so isolating, as if you're emotionally distant from everyone around you.*

Mental Emptiness: The Fog in Your Head

Mental emptiness is when your mind feels cloudy or blank. You might find yourself staring at a screen or page, unable to focus or form coherent thoughts. It's that moment when your brain feels overloaded, yet empty at the same time.

- *Mental emptiness can come from stress, overwork, or long-term fatigue.*

- *It can feel like your brain has switched off, leaving you feeling disconnected from your own thoughts and creativity.*

- *This feeling isn't permanent, but it's important to address the causes so you don't stay stuck in a mental loop.*

This often happens when we're overwhelmed or burned out. The mental clutter becomes so dense that it's hard to find clarity or motivation. And when you can't focus, everything feels more difficult.

Spiritual Emptiness: The Disconnect from Purpose

Spiritual emptiness is that deeper sense of feeling lost, like you're not really sure what your purpose is or if you're on the right path. It doesn't necessarily have to do with religion, but more about feeling disconnected from your true self, your values, or the greater meaning of life.

- *Spiritual emptiness can arise when we feel disconnected from our purpose or our deeper sense of self.*

- *It's a sign that we may need to reassess our goals, values, or the way we approach life.*

- *Reconnecting with your inner beliefs, passions, or even simply slowing down to reflect on what truly matters can help fill this space.*

This type of emptiness is often experienced when you feel like you're just going through life on autopilot, without any real sense of direction or fulfillment.

Clearing Up the Myths:

There are a lot of misconceptions around emptiness that can make it even harder to accept. Let's clear them up:

Myth #1:
"If I feel empty, something's wrong with me.

Reality: Absolutely not. Feeling empty is a normal human experience. It doesn't mean you're broken or defective—it just means that there's something in your emotional, mental, or spiritual life that needs attention.

Myth #2:
"Only weak people feel empty."

Reality: Emptiness doesn't discriminate. It can hit anyone, at any stage in life, no matter how strong or successful they seem. It's part of the human condition, and it doesn't mean you're weak. In fact, acknowledging emptiness and working through it takes great strength.

Myth #3:
"I just need to distract myself, and it'll go away."

Reality: Distractions might offer a temporary escape, but they don't resolve the issue. If you ignore emptiness, it often just comes back stronger. The key is to face it head-on, acknowledge it, and understand what it's telling you.

Myth #4:
"If I don't feel happy all the time, I'm not doing life right."

Reality: Life isn't about constant happiness. We're human, and we go through ups and downs. Feeling empty sometimes doesn't mean you're failing. It's a natural part of the journey, and you can use it to create deeper meaning in your life.

Myth #5:

"Emptiness is a sign that I'll always feel this way."

Reality: Emptiness is temporary, and like all emotions, it passes. It's a sign of a phase or a feeling that needs attention. When you allow yourself to experience it without judgment, you start to see how it shifts and changes, and eventually, it clears.

Myth #6:

"If I don't figure it out fast, I'll never feel whole again."

Reality: There's no rush to fix everything. Healing takes time, and sometimes the process of understanding emptiness and working through it is as important as the outcome. The journey itself can be deeply transformative.

The Societal Stigma Around Emptiness

In a world that glorifies busyness and success, admitting to feelings of emptiness can feel like admitting to failure. Society often equates happiness with external achievements—wealth, career, relationships—and leaves little room for introspection or vulnerability.

This stigma prevents many people from seeking help or even acknowledging their feelings. Instead, they mask their emptiness with distractions like social media, shopping, or constant productivity. But this only deepens the void, as no external solution can fill an internal gap.

To truly address emptiness, we must first challenge the societal narrative that links our worth to our accomplishments. Feeling empty doesn't mean we're broken; it means we're searching for something deeper. By normalizing conversations about emptiness, we create a space for healing and growth.

Emptiness Doesn't Define You

It's essential to understand that emptiness doesn't define who you are. It's simply a phase or a signal that something in your life is out of alignment. Think of it like a pause in your story—an invitation to take a deeper look at what's working and what isn't. Emptiness can be uncomfortable, but it can also be the starting point for something new.

Next time you experience that hollow feeling, remember: it's not the end of the story. It's just a chapter that's asking you to reflect, learn, and grow.

"Emptiness isn't the end of the road; it's the pause before a new beginning, a quiet space where the seeds of change are planted."

CHAPTER 2

What Fills and Empties Us?

"Emptiness isn't random—it's a ripple from the things we've lost, ignored, or over-chased. The good news? We can figure out what's causing it and learn to tip the balance back in our favor."

The Roots of That Hollow Feeling

Have you ever felt like something inside you is just… missing? Like you're going through the motions, but none of it is really sticking? That hollow feeling often has a story behind it—a mix of life's punches and the weight we carry. Let's explore some of the big culprits:

1.Loss – The Pain of Letting Go

Life's losses come in many forms: a breakup, the death of someone we love, losing a job, or watching a dream slip away. These moments don't just leave a gap where something or someone used to be—they make us question what life is about. Loss is like an unexpected guest that leaves behind silence, and we're left trying to fill the space it creates.

2.Burnout – When You're Running on Empty

You know that feeling when you've given and given until there's nothing left? Burnout isn't just about being tired; it's emotional and mental exhaustion. It sneaks in when you pour energy into work, relationships, or responsibilities without taking time to refill your tank. It's like driving a car with the fuel light on, hoping you'll magically make it to the next station. Spoiler: you won't.

3.Loneliness – Surrounded, Yet Alone

Loneliness isn't always about being alone. It's possible to be surrounded by people and still feel like no one truly sees or understands you. The disconnection from others— or even from yourself—can amplify that hollow feeling, turning it into a constant background noise in your life.

The Modern Drains: How the World Makes It Worse

We live in an age where everything is fast, flashy, and filtered. While technology and modern conveniences can help, they also come with a cost.

1.Social Media – The Highlight Reel of Life

Let's be real: most of what you see online is someone's best 10%. The vacations, the career wins, the picture-perfect moments—they create this illusion that everyone has it together except you. You scroll and compare, and before you know it, you're left feeling inadequate.

2.The Comparison Trap

Whether it's the size of someone's paycheck, house, or happiness, we often find ourselves measuring our worth against others. It's exhausting and unfair because we're comparing our behind-the-scenes to their highlight reel.

3.Busyness – The Lie We All Bought Into

How often do you feel guilty for just sitting and doing nothing? We've been conditioned to think that being busy equals being valuable. The constant hustle leaves no room for rest, reflection, or even noticing what's missing.

Reflection: What's Draining You and What's Filling You?

Sometimes, the emptiness inside isn't about what's missing—it's about what's too present. Toxic relationships, pointless routines, self-doubt—these things weigh us down. On the flip side, there are things that refill us, that light us up in a way that feels effortless.

Here's a moment to pause and reflect:

What Drains You?

• Is it overcommitting to things you don't care about?

- Are you giving too much to people who take but don't give back?

- Maybe it's spending too much time on autopilot, doing things that don't excite or inspire you.

What Fills You?

- Think about the last time you felt truly alive—what were you doing?

- Maybe it was having an honest conversation, getting lost in a creative hobby, or just sitting in silence with a good cup of tea.

- What moments make you feel connected to yourself and the world around you?

Key Questions for Reflection

1. Are there parts of your life where you feel stuck or unfulfilled?

2. Do your current habits and routines align with what truly matters to you?

3. Are there relationships that drain more energy than they give?

"Emptiness isn't a sign of failure; it's a doorway. When you take the time to understand what's behind it, you begin to see the path to something greater."

CHAPTER 3

The Beauty of Stillness

"Stillness isn't about doing nothing. It's about making space for everything that truly matters."

Why Stillness Feels So Uncomfortable

Let's be honest—sitting still with your thoughts can feel like stepping into quicksand. Everything you've been ignoring or running from suddenly bubbles up. It's uncomfortable, even scary. But here's the truth: stillness isn't the enemy—it's the doorway to understanding yourself.

- **The Noise in Your Head Gets Louder:** Ever notice how, when you try to sit quietly, your brain starts replaying that embarrassing thing you said five years ago? Or it suddenly reminds you of every errand you forgot to do? This is normal. Stillness makes space for the mental chatter you've been suppressing. But here's the trick: instead of fighting the noise, just let it be. Think of it like background music—you don't have to tune into every note.

- **We're Addicted to Busyness:** In a world where "hustle culture" reigns supreme, sitting still feels like wasting time. But guess what? Busyness doesn't equal success or happiness. Sometimes it's just a distraction from the deeper stuff. Being still is like hitting the pause button on life. It gives you a moment to breathe, reflect, and refocus.

- **Fear of What We'll Find:** Let's face it—sometimes we avoid quiet moments because we're scared of what might come up. Old regrets, buried feelings, or that nagging question, "Am I really happy?" But here's the thing: what you find in the stillness can also set you free.

How Silence and Solitude Help Us Heal

Stillness is often misunderstood as emptiness. But think of it like the ocean. On the surface, it might look calm and quiet, but underneath, there's so much happening. That's what stillness does for your mind and soul—it lets the healing begin.

- **Clarity Loves Quiet:** Have you ever had a great idea pop into your head while you were doing something mundane, like washing dishes or driving? That's because your brain finally had the space to think. Silence clears out the mental clutter, making room for insights and solutions.

- **Loneliness vs. Solitude:** Being alone isn't the same as being lonely. Solitude is a choice—a way to connect with yourself. It's where you get to ask, "What do I really want? What makes me happy?" And sometimes, it's where you realize you've been looking for answers in the wrong places.

- **The Snow Globe Effect:** Picture your mind as a snow globe. When life shakes you up, everything inside gets chaotic and cloudy. But when you sit still, the snow settles. Suddenly, everything becomes clear.

Gentle Ways to Start Sitting with Your Feelings

Stillness doesn't have to mean sitting cross-legged in a dark room, meditating for hours. It's about finding what works for you. Here are a few ideas to ease into it:

1.Start Small with the Five-Minute Pause

If the idea of sitting still freaks you out, begin with just five minutes. Find a quiet spot, set a timer, and close your eyes. Breathe deeply and let your thoughts come and go without judgment. You don't have to "fix" anything—just be present.

2.Use Your Senses to Ground Yourself

Sometimes silence feels overwhelming. Instead, focus on your senses.

- Look around and notice five things you can see.

- Listen for four things you can hear.

- Feel three things (like the texture of your clothes or the chair beneath you).

- Smell two scents.

- Taste one thing, even if it's just the lingering flavor of coffee.

This exercise pulls you out of your head and into the present moment.

3. Write It Out

If sitting still feels impossible, grab a journal and start writing. Let it flow—messy, unfiltered, raw. Write what you're feeling, what's bugging you, or even what you're grateful for. Writing is stillness in motion.

4. Walk, But Slowly

Stillness doesn't always mean staying put. Take a slow, mindful walk. Feel the ground beneath your feet, notice the rustle of leaves, or just focus on your breath as you move.

Finding the Beauty in Being Still

Here's the thing about stillness: It's not something you "master." It's a practice, a gift you give yourself. It's in the quiet moments that you begin to understand who you are beyond the noise and chaos of life.

Stillness teaches us to let go of the need to fix, control, or avoid. It reminds us that healing doesn't happen overnight—it happens in the pauses, the breaths, the moments where we simply let ourselves be.

"Stillness isn't a retreat; it's a return—to yourself, your truth, and your strength."

PART II

Exploring the Space Within

"Within the silent corners of our inner space lies the strength to heal, the clarity to grow, and the courage to embrace who we truly are."

CHAPTER 4

Meeting Yourself Where You Are

"The first step to healing is not to change yourself, but to truly meet yourself—messy emotions and all."

Why We Struggle to Accept Our Feelings

Let's be real—most of us are pros at avoiding our feelings. When sadness creeps in, we binge-watch our favorite shows. When anxiety strikes, we scroll endlessly on social media. Why? Because sitting with our emotions can feel overwhelming, even unbearable.

- **We've Been Taught to Avoid "Negative" Emotions:** Growing up, many of us heard things like, "Don't cry—it's not a big deal," or "Be strong." Over time, we start seeing emotions like sadness, anger, or fear as weaknesses to hide rather than experiences to feel.

- **Judgment Makes It Worse:** When tough feelings show up, our inner critic often follows, whispering things like, "Why are you so sensitive?" or "You shouldn't feel this way." This self-judgment creates a cycle where we not only feel bad, but we also feel bad about feeling bad.

Embracing Your Feelings Without Judgment

Meeting yourself where you are isn't about forcing positivity or pretending everything's okay. It's about saying, *"This is how I feel right now, and that's okay."*

How to Start:

1.Name the Feeling

Instead of running from what you feel, pause and ask yourself:
- "What am I feeling right now?"

- "Where do I feel it in my body?"(Is it a knot in your stomach? A tightness in your chest?) Naming the feeling—whether it's sadness frustration, or worry—helps you acknowledge it without letting it overwhelm you.

2.Remind Yourself: Feelings Are Temporary

No emotion, no matter how intense, lasts forever. Feelings are like waves—they rise, peak, and eventually fade.When you sit with your emotions instead of fighting them, you let them pass naturally.

3.Drop the "Shoulds"

Let go of thoughts like:

- "I shouldn't feel this way."
- "Other people have it worse."

Your emotions are valid, no matter what anyone else is going through.

How Self-Compassion Changes Everything

When you meet yourself with kindness instead of criticism, you create space for healing. Self-compassion isn't about making excuses or avoiding growth; it's about treating yourself like you'd treat a good friend.

Three Steps to Self-Compassion:

1.Recognize That You're Hurting

It's okay to admit you're struggling. Saying something as simple as, *"This is really hard for me,"* can be a powerful way to acknowledge your pain.

2.Remember You're Not Alone

Everyone experiences tough emotions. Remind yourself that feeling this way doesn't make you broken—it makes you human.

3.Be Kind to Yourself

Swap harsh self-talk for encouraging words. Instead of saying, *"Why can't I handle this?"* try, *"I'm doing the best I can right now."*

Exercises to Make Peace with Your Inner World

Small, practical steps can help you start embracing your emotions and meeting yourself where you are.

1.The "Sit and Listen" Practice

• Find a quiet spot and close your eyes.

• Take a few deep breaths and ask yourself, "What do I need to hear right now?"

• Don't try to force an answer—just listen. Maybe it's silence, or maybe it's something your heart has been trying to tell you.

2.Write a Letter to Your Feelings

• Grab a piece of paper and write to the emotion you're feeling.

For example: "Dear anxiety, I see you've shown up again.
I know you're trying to protect me,
but you're making things harder.
Let's figure out how to work together."

• This exercise helps you externalize your feelings and see them as part of your experience, not your entire identity.

3. Create a Self-Compassion Phrase

Think of a comforting statement to repeat when emotions
get tough, like:

  • "It's okay to feel this way."

  • "I am enough, even when I'm struggling."

  • "This feeling doesn't define me."

Acceptance Isn't Giving Up—It's Showing Up

Meeting yourself where you are doesn't mean you're
settling for less. It means you're stepping into the truth of
your experience, even when it's messy or uncomfortable.
Acceptance creates a foundation where real growth can
begin.

You don't have to "fix" yourself or your feelings
overnight. Healing starts with showing up for yourself,
exactly as you are, and saying, *"I'm here, and I'm willing
to try."*

*"When you meet yourself with kindness, you stop running
from the storm and start finding shelter within it."*

CHAPTER 5

Unearthing Hidden Treasures

"What if the very things you think you've lost—strength, joy, and purpose—are just waiting to be rediscovered within you?"

Finding the Gold Beneath the Surface

Life can sometimes feel like it's stripped everything away, leaving us empty. But what if I told you that deep inside, you're still carrying treasures? Strengths, talents, resilience —they're there, buried beneath the weight of stress, fear, or just the grind of everyday life. Think of it like this: you're not broken, you're a treasure chest waiting to be opened.

Sometimes, all it takes is a little digging, a bit of patience, and a willingness to see yourself differently.

Strength: The Quiet Superpower You Forget You Have

Here's a truth we often overlook: strength doesn't always roar. It doesn't have to look like bold action or loud victories. Sometimes, strength whispers. It's in the small, everyday moments you choose to keep going when it feels easier to give up.

Signs You're Stronger Than You Think:

- You're still here, aren't you? That means you've survived every tough moment so far.

- You've shown up for others. Even when your own tank was running low, you've cared.

- You've learned from setbacks. Growth doesn't mean never failing—it means using failure to rise again.

These are quiet victories, but they're powerful. Don't dismiss them.

Small Joys: The Everyday Magic

When life feels overwhelming, it's easy to believe that only big, dramatic changes can make things better. But honestly? Sometimes, it's the tiniest sparks of joy that remind us life isn't all bad.

What Are Small Joys?

• A sunrise that paints the sky in colors you can't even name.

• The smell of your favorite food cooking in the kitchen.

• Laughing at a silly meme that hits way too close to home.

- The way the sun feels on your face during a morning walk.

- A song that makes you want to dance, even if you're in your living room.

Why They Matter:

Small joys are like breadcrumbs leading you back to yourself. They remind you to pause, breathe, and notice the beauty in moments you might otherwise miss.

Gratitude: The Perspective Shifter

Let's be real: gratitude gets a bad rap. It's not about slapping a smile on your face and pretending everything's okay. It's about balancing the bad with the good, noticing the light even when it feels dim.

Why Practice Gratitude?

- It helps you reframe your focus. Instead of spiraling into negativity, it nudges you to see the good.

- It builds emotional resilience, making it easier to bounce back from challenges.

- It's a way of saying, "Hey, life's not perfect, but this moment? It's enough."

Start small. Think of one thing—just one—that made you smile today. That's gratitude in action.

Reflecting on What Matters

Self-discovery isn't about uncovering some grand, hidden truth about yourself. It's about reconnecting with the simple things that make you feel alive and whole.

Try These Journaling Prompts:

1.What's one thing I've done recently that I'm proud of, even if it's small?

2.What are three things I love doing but haven't made time for?

3.When was the last time I felt truly at peace, and what was I doing?

4.What's something I've overcome that proves I'm stronger than I give myself credit for?

Write freely, no filters. This is your space to explore.

Growth Happens One Treasure at a Time

Here's the thing about life: you don't have to have it all figured out. You don't need to be a shining example of perfection. You just have to start small, rediscovering the pieces of yourself that bring you joy, strength, and hope.

"You are your own treasure chest. Everything you need—resilience, courage, joy—is already inside. All you have to do is look within."

CHAPTER 6

Redefining Your Purpose

"Purpose isn't something you find—it's something you create, piece by piece, with every choice you make."

What Gives Your Life Meaning?

Let's get real—this whole idea of "purpose" can feel overwhelming, right? Like you're supposed to have some grand plan or life mission figured out by now. Newsflash: most people don't. And guess what? That's totally fine.

Purpose isn't about having all the answers or following a perfect roadmap. It's more like finding a trail of breadcrumbs along the way. Some lead you to exciting new places, while others might feel like dead ends. But every step teaches you something.

Think about it: What makes you feel alive? What moments make time fly? Purpose is often hiding in those little things—things that feel so simple, you might not even realize how important they are.

Redefining What Purpose Means

Before we dive deeper, let's debunk some of the biggest myths about purpose:
1.It Has to Be Big and Grand.

Nope! Purpose isn't about saving the world or becoming a billionaire (though, hey, if that's your thing, go for it). It could be as simple as making people smile, creating art, or being the glue that holds your family together.

2.It's Only About Your Career.

Wrong again. Purpose doesn't have to be tied to your job. Your sense of fulfillment can come from your relationships, hobbies, or even just how you treat others.

3.It's a One-Time Discovery.

Here's the thing: your purpose isn't set in stone. It changes as you grow. What felt meaningful five years ago might not resonate anymore—and that's okay. Purpose is more like a playlist than a single track.

Why Does Finding Purpose Feel So Hard?

Let's talk about the elephant in the room: *fear.*

Fear of Failure

We're so scared of messing up that we sometimes don't even start. But failure isn't the end—it's part of the process. Every stumble teaches you something.

Fear of Judgment

What will people think? Let's be honest—people will always have opinions. But their judgments don't define your life. Only you get to do that.

Fear of Not Knowing

It's terrifying to not have everything figured out. But guess what? Nobody does. Uncertainty is where the magic happens—it's where growth lives.

Taking the First Steps

Redefining your purpose isn't about waking up tomorrow with your entire life planned out. It's about starting small, exploring what feels good, and allowing yourself to evolve.

Step 1: Look Back

Think about a time when you felt truly happy or alive. What were you doing? Who were you with? Those moments can be clues to what matters most to you.

Step 2: Notice What Fills You Up

Start paying attention to what brings you joy or peace—
and what drains you. The things that energize you are
often tied to your sense of purpose.

Step 3: Experiment Without Pressure

Try something new, revisit an old hobby, or explore a
passion you've put on the back burner. It doesn't have to
be perfect or even permanent.

Journaling Prompts to Help You Explore

- What's something you've always wanted to try but never
  had the courage to?

- When do you feel most like yourself?

- If money and time weren't an issue, how would you
  spend your days?

- What kind of impact do you want to leave on the world?

Purpose Isn't Always About Big Things

Here's the truth: your purpose might not feel monumental.
It's not always about building an empire or changing the
world. Sometimes, it's just about the little things—being
kind, creating something beautiful, or making someone's
day better.

Purpose is in the way you show up, the connections you build, and the love you share. It's about making the most of who you are, right here, right now.

So, let's stop overcomplicating purpose. It's not a finish line or a prize—it's a journey. It's about discovering what makes your heart sing and finding joy in the process of figuring it out.

"Purpose isn't a destination. It's a feeling, a choice, and a collection of moments that make your life meaningful."

PART III

Transforming Emptiness into Strength

CHAPTER 7

Turning the Quiet into Power

"When life gets too loud, it's in the quiet where we often find our strength—not by drowning out the emptiness, but by listening to what it's trying to say."

Let's Redefine the Quiet

For most of us, quietness can feel…awkward. It's like that uncomfortable silence in a conversation where nobody knows what to say. But what if I told you that this quiet isn't something to fear or fill up with noise? It's a space— a blank slate waiting for you to paint something beautiful on it.

Life can feel overwhelming at times, and when that overwhelming feeling fades, we're often left with silence. That silence can seem like loneliness, but in reality, it's an opportunity to dig deep and discover what we're truly capable of.

Think of the quiet as your reset button. It's not a punishment. It's your chance to stop, breathe, and start again.

Why We Fear Quiet

Let's be real—quiet can be uncomfortable because it forces us to face things we'd rather avoid. You know, those thoughts that pop up when you're lying in bed at night or taking a long walk alone. The "What am I doing with my life?" kind of thoughts.

But here's the thing: running away from them doesn't make them disappear. Ignoring your feelings is like putting tape over your car's check engine light—it doesn't fix the problem.

Why Quiet Feels Uncomfortable:

1.It Exposes Us

Quiet moments reveal what's really going on inside. They strip away distractions and leave us alone with our true thoughts.

2.It Demands Reflection

When there's no noise, we start to question things. Am I happy? Am I on the right path? And those questions can be scary.

3.It Forces Growth

Growth often comes from discomfort. Sitting in the quiet is like going to the gym for your mind—it might feel tough at first, but it makes you stronger

How the Quiet Becomes Powerful

The quiet can be a superpower if you learn how to use it. When you stop fighting it and start embracing it, something amazing happens: the silence turns into clarity, and the emptiness becomes a wellspring of creativity, motivation, and strength.

Think about it this way: some of the most innovative ideas and beautiful creations came from people who felt empty. Why? Because that emptiness creates space to dream, to think, and to build.

How Quiet Unlocks Potential:

• It Clears the Noise

When the outside world gets too loud, quiet moments help you reconnect with what truly matters.

• It Fuels Creativity

When there's nothing to distract you, your mind starts coming up with solutions, ideas, and possibilities.

• It Builds Resilience

Sitting with your feelings instead of running from them strengthens your ability to face challenges head-on.

Finding Creativity in the Quiet

Let me tell you a story. There was a man who lost his job and spent months feeling useless. Instead of wallowing in self-pity, he started sketching. Those sketches turned into designs, and those designs eventually became the foundation of his own business.

He didn't plan it. He didn't have some grand strategy. He simply let the quiet guide him toward something he loved.

How to Tap Into Creativity:

1.Start Small

You don't have to write a novel or invent the next big thing. Begin with something simple, like doodling, writing a poem, or rearranging your living space.

2.Follow Your Curiosity

What's something you've always wanted to try? Painting? Gardening? Making your own playlists? Let curiosity lead the way.

3.Be Okay with "Bad"

Not everything you create has to be a masterpiece. The act of creating itself is where the magic happens.

Helping Others: A Surprising Source of Strength

One of the most unexpected ways to turn emptiness into power is by focusing on someone else. It sounds counterintuitive, but when you're feeling stuck, helping others can give you a sense of purpose and connection that's hard to find on your own.

Why Helping Helps You:

• It Shifts Your Focus

Instead of being consumed by your own struggles, you start to see how you can make a difference in someone else's life.

• It Builds Connection

When you lend a hand, you create bonds and relationships that fill your heart.

• It Reminds You of Your Strengths

Seeing how your actions help others can remind you of the value you bring to the world.

Real-Life Transformations

Need proof? Here are a few examples of how people turned their quiet moments into something incredible:

1.The Chef Who Found His Calling

After a painful breakup, one man started cooking as a way to cope with his emotions. That hobby turned into a full-fledged career, and now he owns a thriving restaurant.

2.The Writer Who Found Her Voice

A woman dealing with burnout began journaling to process her feelings. Over time, those journal entries evolved into a book that's inspired thousands.

3.The Activist Who Created Change

Feeling empty after losing her job, a woman began volunteering at a local shelter. She discovered a passion for advocacy and eventually started her own nonprofit.

Turning the Quiet into Motivation

Ready to start? Here are some simple, actionable steps to turn your quiet moments into something powerful:

1.Acknowledge the Quiet

Don't run from it. Sit with it. Let yourself feel the discomfort—it's the first step to transformation.

2.Ask Yourself Questions

What am I feeling right now? What do I need? What's one small thing I can do today to move forward?

3.Take Action, No Matter How Small

Write one paragraph. Take one photo. Reach out to one friend. Small actions build momentum.

4.Celebrate Progress

Even if it's tiny, every step forward is worth celebrating. Growth happens in the little moments.

A Quiet Power

The quiet within you isn't empty—it's powerful. It's a space for new beginnings, fresh ideas, and meaningful connections. Embrace it, and you might be surprised by what you're capable of.

"Your quiet moments hold the seeds of your greatest potential. What will you grow?"

CHAPTER 8

Building Connections That Heal

"Connection is the antidote to emptiness—it doesn't erase the hollow space but fills it with meaning, trust, and warmth."

Why Connections Matter

Let's be real: life feels easier when we have someone to lean on. Whether it's calling a friend to rant about your day or having a heart-to-heart with a loved one, meaningful connections have a magical way of making us feel grounded. But when emptiness creeps in, the first thing we often do is pull back from people. It's like we're trying to protect our fragile inner world by keeping everyone out. Spoiler alert: that usually makes things worse.

Here's the deal—relationships, even the messy ones, are what help us heal. They're not about perfection or grand gestures; they're about the little things that remind you you're not alone in this big, chaotic world.

The Power of Connection

Let's face it: when life feels heavy, our first instinct is often to isolate ourselves. It's like when you're dealing with a broken heart, and your playlist is suddenly filled with sad songs, the curtains are drawn, and the world feels distant. But here's the thing—healing doesn't happen in a vacuum. It happens in connection.

Relationships, both with others and yourself, play a vital role in finding strength. They're not just about feeling "better" but about rediscovering the human need to share, love, and grow. Let's explore how meaningful relationships—whether with loved ones, friends, or even your inner self—can mend the cracks and offer a sense of belonging.

The Role of Relationships in Finding Strength

Imagine this: you're walking a tightrope, and below you is a safety net. That net? It's your connections. They won't stop you from wobbling, but they'll catch you when you fall.

Here's why relationships are your secret weapon:

- **Perspective:** Sometimes, we get stuck in our own heads, overthinking and spiraling. A conversation with a friend can offer clarity you didn't know you needed.

- **Support:** Whether it's a hug, a pep talk, or just someone listening, connections give us the strength to keep going.

- **Energy Boost:** A good laugh with someone you love can do wonders for your mood and motivation.

Why Do We Struggle to Connect?

Let's be honest—it's not always easy to reach out, especially when you're feeling empty. Maybe you don't want to "burden" anyone, or you've been burned by toxic relationships in the past. Or maybe, you've just gotten used to being your own island.

Here's what often holds us back:

- **Fear of Rejection:** What if they don't understand? What if they don't care? These "what ifs" can be paralyzing.

- **Vulnerability is Scary:** Opening up feels like handing someone the keys to your heart and hoping they don't drop them.

- **Past Hurt:** Old wounds from broken trust or toxic dynamics can make it hard to believe in the power of connection again.

But here's the truth: no relationship is perfect, and some will disappoint you. Yet, the right ones—the ones rooted in love, respect, and understanding—are worth the risk.

Building Trust: One Step at a Time

Trust doesn't happen overnight. It's like planting a seed and watering it little by little. Some tips for building or rebuilding trust:

- **Consistency:** Show up when you say you will. Even small actions, like replying to messages or remembering someone's birthday, matter.

- **Honesty:** Be real. Share your thoughts, even if they're messy or imperfect. People connect to authenticity, not polished facades.

- **Patience:** Trust takes time. Don't rush it. Let it grow naturally.

Vulnerability: Your Superpower in Disguise

Let's talk about vulnerability—it's uncomfortable, but it's also the gateway to deeper relationships. Think about the moments when someone shared their struggles with you. Didn't it make you feel closer to them? That's the power of vulnerability.

Here's how to practice being open:

- **Start Small:** Share something you're comfortable with, like a recent challenge at work or a funny mistake you made.

- **Be Present:** When someone shares with you, really listen. Put away your phone and give them your full attention.

- **Celebrate the Brave Moments:** Every time you open up, acknowledge your courage. Vulnerability isn't weakness; it's strength.

Activities to Deepen Connections

Building connections isn't just about talking; it's about creating moments that matter. Here are some fun, simple ways to strengthen your bonds:

For Loved Ones:

- **Memory Lane:** Share stories from your past—how you met, your funniest moments together, or even the struggles you've overcome.

- **Unplugged Time:** Spend time together without screens. Cook a meal, go for a walk, or play a board game.

- **Gratitude Practice:** Take turns telling each other what you appreciate. It's a quick way to feel closer.

For Yourself:

- **Solo Adventures:** Treat yourself to a solo movie night, hike, or coffee date. Learn to enjoy your own company.

- **Journaling:** Write letters to yourself. What would you say to comfort or encourage yourself?

- **Mindful Moments:** Take five minutes a day to sit in silence, focusing on your breath. It's a simple way to reconnect with yourself.

Letting Go of What Doesn't Serve You

Not every relationship is worth holding onto. Some connections drain you more than they fill you. Here's how to tell if it's time to let go:

- **They Constantly Bring You Down:** If someone's always negative or dismissive, it's okay to step back.

- **It's One-Sided: Healthy relationships involve give and take.** If you're always the giver, it might be time to reevaluate.

- **You Feel Unsafe or Unvalued: Trust your instincts.** If a relationship feels toxic, prioritize your well-being.

Ask yourself:

> - Does this person lift me up or pull me down?
>
> - Am I always the one giving without receiving?
>
> - Do I feel safe and valued in this relationship?

Letting go isn't easy, but it creates space for relationships that truly nurture you.

Rebuilding the Connection with Yourself

At the heart of it all is your relationship with yourself. How can you expect to connect deeply with others if you're disconnected from your own feelings and needs?

Here's how to strengthen your bond with yourself:

- **Daily Check-Ins:** Ask yourself, "How am I feeling today? What do I need?"

- **Celebrate Wins:** Big or small, acknowledge your achievements.

- **Be Kind to Yourself:** Speak to yourself the way you'd talk to a dear friend.

The Ripple Effect of Connection

Connection is a two-way street. When you open your heart to others, you inspire them to do the same. It creates a ripple effect, spreading warmth and understanding in a world that often feels cold.

"Healing starts when we realize that we're all walking this path together—sometimes hand in hand, sometimes side by side, but never truly alone."

CHAPTER 9

Creating a Life You Love

"Life is less about finding yourself and more about creating a version of yourself and your days that you truly enjoy waking up to."

What Does "Creating a Life You Love" Really Mean?

Let's be real. The phrase "create a life you love" is tossed around like confetti, and it often feels as vague as it does inspiring. Are we supposed to overhaul our entire existence? Move to Bali? Start a million-dollar business? Honestly, no. Creating a life you love doesn't require some dramatic, Instagram-worthy transformation.

It's about crafting a life that feels meaningful to you. A life where your daily choices—big or small—align with your values, bring you joy, and give you a sense of purpose. It's about designing your days to feel like they belong to you, not just something you're surviving through.

Why Do Routines Matter in Building a Life You Love?

We're creatures of habit, whether we like it or not. Our days are made up of tiny decisions and repeated actions.

And here's the secret: when you intentionally design those small moments, they add up to something beautiful.

Think of routines as your daily anchor. They don't have to be rigid or boring; instead, they create a rhythm that lets you feel grounded, focused, and at peace.

- **Routines Save Brain Power:** Ever notice how exhausting it is to make a million tiny decisions each day? "What do I eat? When do I exercise? Should I call this person back now or later?" A solid routine takes the guesswork out of your day, leaving you more energy for the fun and creative stuff.

- **They Build Momentum:** Consistent habits are like compounding interest. Small daily actions, like journaling or meditating for five minutes, lead to big changes over time.

- **They Help You Stay Present:** A thoughtful routine creates space for mindfulness. When you know what to expect, you can actually slow down and enjoy the process.

Step 1: Define What "Loving Your Life" Looks Like to YOU

The first step to creating a life you love is to figure out what that actually means for you. Forget about society's expectations or what your favorite influencer is doing.

Ask yourself:

• What makes me feel alive?

• When do I feel most at peace?

• Who or what brings me joy?

• What values do I want to prioritize (e.g., connection, health, creativity, adventure)?

Your version of a joyful life might look like quiet mornings with a cup of tea and a good book, or it might be filled with travel and spontaneity. The beauty is—it's yours to define.

Step 2: Build a Routine Around Growth, Peace, and Joy

When you're clear on what matters to you, it's time to weave those elements into your daily life. Think of it as creating a routine that balances three key pillars: growth, peace, and joy.

Growth: Your Stretch Zone

Growth is about becoming the best version of yourself—not in a hustle-culture way, but in a way that feels inspiring and empowering.

- **Morning Mindset Ritual:** Spend five minutes in the morning setting an intention. Ask yourself, "What's one thing I can do today to move closer to my goals?"

- **Continuous Learning:** Read a book, listen to a podcast, or take a short online course. Even 10 minutes a day adds up.

- **Reflect and Adapt:** At the end of the week, ask yourself what worked, what didn't, and how you can improve. Growth is about learning as you go.

Peace: Your Recharge Zone

In a world that glorifies being busy, creating moments of peace is a radical act. Peace doesn't just happen—you have to cultivate it.

- **Mindful Moments:** Take a few minutes to breathe deeply, stretch, or simply sit in silence.

- **Disconnect to Reconnect:** Set boundaries with your phone. Try a "tech-free hour" where you focus on being fully present.

- **Evening Wind-Down Ritual:** End your day with calming activities, like journaling about your wins or reading something uplifting.

Joy: Your Spark Zone

Joy doesn't have to be extravagant. It's found in the small, beautiful moments that make your heart feel lighter.

- **Celebrate Tiny Wins:** Did you make it through a tough day? High-five yourself. Every step forward deserves recognition.

- **Play Every Day:** Dance in your kitchen, sing in the shower, or doodle on a notepad. Play is essential for adults, too.

- **Gratitude Practice:** Before bed, jot down three things that made you smile that day. Gratitude rewires your brain to focus on the positive.

Step 3: Tools to Help You Stay on Track

Let's be real: sticking to a routine isn't always easy. Life gets messy, and that's okay. Here are some tools to help you stay consistent:

- **Habit Trackers:** Apps like Habitica or Streaks can gamify your routines and make them fun.

- **Gratitude Journals:** Writing down what you're thankful for shifts your focus from what's lacking to what's abundant.

- **Guided Meditations**: Apps like Headspace or Insight Timer can help you find your calm amidst the chaos.

Step 4: Embrace Small Steps, Big Impact

Here's the thing: you don't need to overhaul your life overnight. In fact, trying to do too much at once often backfires. The real magic lies in taking small, consistent steps every day.

- **Example 1:** Start your day with a single glass of water before coffee.

- **Example 2:** Commit to 10 minutes of journaling or stretching.

- **Example 3:** Smile at a stranger or compliment a friend —it spreads joy and builds connection.

Every small step adds up. Over time, you'll look back and realize how far you've come.

Step 5: When Things Don't Go as Planned

Life isn't perfect, and neither are we. There will be days when your routine falls apart or when you feel like you're taking two steps back. And that's okay.

- **Be Gentle with Yourself:** Progress isn't linear. Remind yourself that it's about effort, not perfection.

- **Reset and Refocus:** If you fall off track, don't beat yourself up. Simply start again.

- **Celebrate the Effort:** Even showing up imperfectly is better than not trying at all.

Designing Your Masterpiece

Creating a life you love isn't a destination—it's a daily practice. It's about finding meaning in the small moments, taking intentional steps toward growth, and embracing the messiness of being human.

So start where you are. Show up, experiment, and give yourself permission to design a life that feels uniquely yours.

"Every choice you make today is a brushstroke on the canvas of your life. Paint boldly, joyfully, and with love."

PART IV

The Journey to Inner Strength

"The journey from emptiness to strength isn't about filling the void; it's about discovering the power that's always been there, waiting to be unlocked."

CHAPTER 10

From Emptiness to Empowerment

"Sometimes, life brings you to your knees—not to break you, but to remind you how strong you can be when you rise again."

A Journey of Full Circles

We're at the final chapter, and I hope you feel like you've come full circle. Remember where we started? Back in the haze of feeling empty, unsure, and lost? Now, here we are, talking about empowerment. This is where we flip the narrative. This is where emptiness, once so daunting, becomes a strength you carry forward.

But before we dive in, let's take a moment. Pause. Breathe. Let this be a quiet moment of reflection. Think about how far you've come—not just in reading this book, but in your own life.

Because here's the truth: you've already been transforming. Every chapter you've read, every thought you've explored, every emotion you've faced has been a step toward reclaiming your strength.

We've walked through the trenches of emptiness together
—questioned it, sat with it, and even learned to appreciate
it. Now, it's time to talk about how that emptiness
transforms into something extraordinary. Because let's
face it, no one wants to carry around a void forever, right?

Now let me share a story—*my story*—about how
emptiness tested me in ways I never expected, and how it
eventually became my greatest teacher.

The Day Life Knocked Me Down

It all began during my engineering entrance preparation
days. If you've ever prepped for a big exam, you'll know
how intense it gets—your world shrinks to books, study
schedules, and mock tests. My first attempt went well
enough: I scored more than 93 percentile. But that wasn't
enough for me.

I decided to take a drop year to aim even higher.

That year was a grind like no other. Late nights, early
mornings, sacrificing social life—all for that one day, that
one exam. I gave it everything. I poured my heart, my
energy, my very identity into those books. The dream of
success kept me going, and I could almost see it: walking
out of the exam hall knowing I'd crushed it.

But then life threw a curveball. On the day of the exam, I
found myself in a hospital bed instead of the exam hall. A

sudden illness had taken me down at the worst possible time. My chance was gone.

When I realized I couldn't take the exam, it felt like the world had caved in. Months of effort, dedication, and sacrifice—all gone in an instant. I cried. I yelled at the universe. I felt like a failure, like everything I'd worked for had been stolen from me.

The Weight of Emptiness

The weeks that followed were some of the hardest of my life. I felt hollow inside, like a part of me had just disappeared. It wasn't just about the exam anymore—it was about the identity I'd tied to it.

- **I felt directionless.** If not this, then what?

- **I felt alone.** Even surrounded by people, the emptiness was louder than ever.

- **I felt defeated.** Like I'd let myself and everyone else down.

This is the kind of emptiness that eats at you, that makes you question everything. And let me tell you, it's not easy to sit with those feelings.

The Turning Point

But then something remarkable happened. My parents, my loved ones—they stood by me in ways I can't even describe. They didn't just offer me words of comfort; they reminded me of who I was beyond that exam. They showed me that my worth wasn't tied to a single test or achievement.

It wasn't an overnight transformation. It never is. But little by little, I started to rebuild myself.

Here's what I realized:

- **Emptiness isn't a dead end; it's a blank slate.** It feels awful, sure, but it's also an opportunity to start fresh.

- **Failure isn't final.** Sometimes, it's just a redirection to something better.

- **Strength doesn't always roar.** Sometimes, it's as simple as getting out of bed, taking a breath, and trying again.

Turning Emptiness into Strength

I decided to channel that emptiness into action. I prepared for another exam—not to prove anything to anyone, but because I knew I wasn't done yet. And this time, I got into one of my dream colleges.

Looking back, I realize that my lowest moment became the foundation for my greatest growth. The emptiness I felt wasn't just a void—it was a space where I could rebuild myself stronger than before.

Practical Steps for Turning Emptiness into Empowerment

Now, let's talk about you. How can you take your own feelings of emptiness and turn them into strength? Here's a roadmap:

1.Sit With the Silence

Don't rush to fill the void with distractions. Sit with it, listen to it. Sometimes, the silence holds the answers you've been avoiding.

2.Redefine Success

Ask yourself: what truly matters to you? Strip away society's expectations and focus on what feels meaningful to you.

3.Reconnect with Your "Why"

Find that spark inside you—the thing that makes you want to get up in the morning. It doesn't have to be grand. Even small joys count.

4.Build a Support System

Lean on the people who love you. Let them in. Vulnerability isn't a weakness; it's a bridge.

5.Celebrate the Small Wins

Progress isn't always flashy. Every little step forward deserves recognition.

6.Turn Pain into Purpose

Use your experiences to fuel something positive. Whether it's creativity, helping others, or pursuing a passion, let that emptiness become your motivation.

A New Chapter

As we close this book, I want to leave you with a simple thought: your journey doesn't end here. In fact, it's just beginning.

Life will continue to throw challenges your way—that's inevitable. But now, you know something many people don't: emptiness isn't your enemy. It's your canvas, your pause button, your secret weapon.

So, here's to you:

> • To your courage in facing the tough times.

• To your strength in rebuilding after the fall.

• To the incredible person you're becoming.

The silent space within you isn't empty anymore. It's full of potential, resilience, and the power to create a life you love.
Now go out there and write your next chapter. Make it one worth reading.

"What lies behind us and what lies before us are tiny matters compared to what lies within us."

Conclusion: From Emptiness to Strength

As we close this chapter of your journey, it's important to reflect on just how far you've come—from a place of emptiness to one of strength. The path wasn't easy, and there were times when you probably felt lost, unsure, or overwhelmed. But here you are, stronger, more self-aware, and ready to embrace whatever life throws your way.

Remember, the emptiness you once feared was never a sign of weakness—it was the space where transformation happened. It was in that quiet, still space that you discovered parts of yourself you never knew existed: your resilience, your creativity, and your ability to keep going even when things seemed impossible.

From Emptiness to Empowerment:

You didn't just sit idly by while life knocked you down—you used every challenge as an opportunity to grow. Each setback became a stepping stone, each moment of doubt turned into a lesson. You learned that emptiness wasn't something to fear but something to embrace and work through. It's like you've been carving your own path, one step at a time, building strength from what once felt like a void.

Your Strength is Your Story:

Your journey, just like everyone's, is unique. But the one thing that unites us all is our capacity to turn pain into power, emptiness into purpose. You've made it through your toughest days, and every trial, every difficult moment, has led you here—to this place of clarity, purpose, and strength.

Now, as you move forward, don't forget the lessons you've learned from your emptiness. Keep in mind that growth doesn't happen overnight. It's an ongoing process. You'll encounter bumps along the way, but each bump is a chance to practice what you've learned.

A Reminder: The Journey Never Ends:

The truth is, this isn't the end of your story. It's just a chapter. There will be more challenges, more changes, and more moments where you might feel a little empty. But that's okay. Now you know that emptiness isn't a dead end —it's an opportunity for new beginnings.

As you continue to live with intention, build meaningful connections, and follow your dreams, remember that your strength lies not in avoiding emptiness but in accepting it, learning from it, and using it to fuel your journey. Embrace stillness. Embrace growth. Embrace the fact that every step forward, no matter how small, is a victory.

You've turned emptiness into your strength, and that's something no one can take from you.

So, go on. Keep creating, keep growing, and keep believing in yourself. The best is yet to come.

Miscellaneous

The Art of Starting Over

*"Every ending carries the seed of a new beginning.
Sometimes, you just need the courage to plant it."*

Why Start Over?

Let's be real: starting over is scary. Whether it's rebuilding
your life after a setback, stepping away from something
that's not working, or simply realizing you need a new
direction—it's never easy. But here's the twist: it's also
one of the most powerful things you can do for yourself.

Think about it this way: every time you start over, you're
giving yourself permission to grow, to evolve, to become
something—or someone—better. It's like hitting the reset
button on a video game. Sure, you might lose a little
progress, but now you've got all this new knowledge to
play smarter.

When Life Feels Like a Blank Page

You know that feeling when you're staring at a blank page,
whether it's for a new project, a new job, or even just
figuring out what's next? It's intimidating. The
possibilities are endless, but so are the doubts:

- "What if I mess this up again?"
- "What if I'm not good enough?"
- "What if it's too late?"

But here's the thing about blank pages: they're full of potential. They're your chance to tell a new story, to write a different ending.

The Beauty of Beginners

Being a beginner isn't something to be ashamed of—it's a superpower. Beginners ask questions, try new things, and don't get stuck in "how things are supposed to be."

Here are a few perks of starting over:

1.Freedom to Redefine Yourself

You're not tied to old labels or expectations. Starting fresh means you get to choose who you want to be.

2.Clarity from Experience

Every setback you've faced has taught you something. Now you're wiser, more resilient, and better equipped to move forward.

3.Room for Creativity

Starting over opens up space for new ideas, hobbies, or passions you might have ignored before.

Steps to Embrace a Fresh Start

Let's break it down. Here's how you can make starting over a little less terrifying and a lot more empowering:

1.Acknowledge the Loss

It's okay to grieve what you're leaving behind, whether it's a failed dream, a broken relationship, or an old version of yourself. Feel it, honor it, and then let it go.

2.Reflect Without Judgment

What worked? What didn't? Think of this as a life audit—not to criticize yourself but to understand where you are and where you want to go.

3.Set Tiny Goals

You don't have to figure it all out at once. Focus on small, manageable steps.

•If you're starting a new career, maybe your first step is just updating your resume.

•If you're rebuilding your confidence, start with one positive affirmation a day.

4.Surround Yourself with Positivity

Whether it's people, books, podcasts, or even your social media feed, make sure your environment supports your growth.

5.Embrace the Awkward Phase

You're going to stumble, and that's okay. Progress isn't linear, and perfection isn't the goal.

6.Celebrate Progress

Every step forward, no matter how small, deserves recognition. Treat yourself like you'd cheer on a friend.

A Personal Story

When I decided to start over after missing my exam due to illness, I felt lost. I questioned everything: my abilities, my future, my worth. But starting over taught me something unexpected—it wasn't about what I had lost but what I still had within me.

The process wasn't glamorous. It was messy, full of self-doubt, and sometimes exhausting. But every small victory—a day spent studying without breaking down, a meaningful conversation with a loved one—reminded me that I was rebuilding something stronger.

The Power of Resilience

Resilience doesn't mean you never fall; it means you keep getting back up. It's about finding strength in the small moments:

•That first cup of tea in the morning that reminds you life is still beautiful.

•The smile you give yourself in the mirror, even when you're not feeling it.

•The tiny spark of hope that whispers, "You can do this."

Starting over isn't a sign of weakness. It's a testament to your courage, your adaptability, and your endless potential.

Practical Exercises to Help You Start Over

Here are a few activities to help you embrace your fresh start:

1.Vision Board

Grab some magazines, scissors, and glue. Create a visual representation of what you want your new chapter to look like.

2.Letter to Your Future Self

Write a letter to the person you're becoming. What do you hope they'll achieve? How do you want them to feel?

3.Anchor Ritual

Create a daily ritual that grounds you. It could be journaling, a morning walk, or even just lighting a candle and reflecting for a few minutes.

A Thought

Starting over isn't about erasing the past. It's about taking the lessons you've learned, the strength you've gained, and using them to build something even better.

As you step into this new chapter, remember:

- You are not defined by your failures or your past.

- You are stronger than you realize.

- You have the power to create a life you love, one small step at a time.

"The magic of life isn't in avoiding endings; it's in daring to begin again."

The Law of Karma – What Goes Around, Comes Around

"What you sow, you shall reap."
— Ancient Wisdom

Understanding the Law of Karma

Karma is one of those concepts that might seem spiritual or philosophical at first glance, but it's really a simple idea: the energy you put into the world—whether positive or negative—comes back to you. It's like a boomerang, except you don't always know when it'll hit you, but you can be sure it will.

This chapter isn't about suggesting you need to do good just to get good in return, but rather, it's about realizing that the choices we make, the energy we give out, and the intentions behind our actions can shape our lives.

How Karma Works in Daily Life

•**Positive Karma:** When you make a conscious effort to be kind, generous, or thoughtful, you're putting out good energy. You'll find that, over time, people treat you with kindness and your life flows with ease.

•**Negative Karma:** On the flip side, when you act with anger, jealousy, or manipulation, you're sending negative energy into the world. While you might get away with it for a while, eventually, the consequences catch up. *The law of karma isn't about punishment or reward; it's about balance. It's the universe's way of maintaining equilibrium.*

Karma in Relationships

Think about how relationships work. Ever notice how when you're genuinely kind and compassionate, people around you seem to reflect that same kindness? It's because the energy you give off invites a similar energy in return. On the other hand, being rude or selfish can lead to resentment and distance.

How to Use the Law of Karma to Your Advantage

1.Be Mindful of Your Actions

Every choice you make has a ripple effect. So before reacting or making decisions, consider the energy you're sending out. Are you acting with love, patience, and understanding, or are you acting out of frustration or ego?

2.Practice Gratitude

Show gratitude not only for the positive things but also for the lessons you learn from tough situations. Gratitude shifts your energy and attracts more things to be grateful for.

3.Give Without Expectation

Do good deeds without expecting anything in return. This shifts the focus from "What's in it for me?" to "How can I contribute to the world?"

4.Let Go of Anger

Holding on to anger only harms you. Forgiving others—and yourself—creates positive energy and releases negative karma.

"Karma is not a punishment; it's a reflection of your actions."

Productivity Tips – Getting More Done Without Losing Your Mind

"You don't have to be great to start, but you have to start to be great."
— Zig Ziglar

Why Productivity Matters

You know that feeling when you've been busy all day, but at the end of it, you feel like you've done nothing? Yeah, we've all been there. Productivity isn't just about doing more; it's about doing the right things, focusing on what truly moves you forward, and making your time count.

Here are some tips to help you focus and get stuff done without feeling overwhelmed:

1. Prioritize Like a Pro

Ask yourself, What will give me the biggest return on my time? The 80/20 Rule, also known as the Pareto Principle, suggests that 80% of your results come from just 20% of your efforts. Focus on the small things that really matter.

2. Time Block Like a Boss

Instead of having an endless to-do list, try time-blocking your day. Set aside specific chunks of time for certain tasks. This helps you avoid multitasking (which is actually counterproductive) and lets you focus on one thing at a time.

3. Use the Pomodoro Technique

The Pomodoro Technique is simple: Work for 25 minutes, then take a 5-minute break. After four "Pomodoros," take a longer break (15–30 minutes). This helps you stay focused without burning out.

4. Eliminate Distractions

The easiest way to be productive is to remove distractions. Put your phone on Do Not Disturb, close unnecessary tabs on your browser, and create a workspace that's free of clutter.

5. Celebrate Small Wins

Productivity isn't just about big wins. Celebrate the small stuff too! Whether it's checking off a small task or staying focused for an hour, each step counts and builds momentum.

"Focus on being productive instead of busy."
— *Tim Ferriss*

Overcoming Procrastination – A Fight We All Face

"Procrastination is the art of keeping up with yesterday."
— Don Marquis

Why Do We Procrastinate?

Let's be honest: we've all put things off. It's natural to avoid tasks that feel overwhelming or uncomfortable. But procrastination isn't just about laziness—it's often a sign of fear, perfectionism, or even lack of clarity.

Common Reasons We Procrastinate:

1.Fear of Failure

We delay because we're afraid of doing something wrong or not doing it perfectly.

2.Overwhelm

Large tasks seem daunting, so we avoid starting them altogether.

3.Lack of Motivation

If we don't see an immediate reward or if the task isn't exciting, we tend to delay.

Methods to Overcome Procrastination

1.Break It Down

Big tasks often seem impossible, but when you break them down into small, manageable steps, they become much more doable.

2.Set a Timer

Try the Pomodoro Technique we discussed earlier. It tricks your brain into thinking, "Hey, I only have to work for 25 minutes!"

3.The 5-Minute Rule

Tell yourself you only need to work for five minutes. Often, the hardest part is starting. Once you're in motion, you'll keep going.

4.Visualize Success

Picture how great it'll feel to cross that task off your list. Visualizing the end result can motivate you to take the first step.

"You don't have to be great to start, but you have to start to be great."
— Zig Ziglar

The Power of Habit – How Small Changes Create Big Results

"Success is the sum of small efforts, repeated day in and day out."
— *Robert Collier*

The Science of Habits

Did you know that the average person spends around 90% of their day on autopilot? Yep, the stuff you do without thinking—brushing your teeth, grabbing a cup of coffee, scrolling through your phone—those are habits.

So, what if you could make your habits work for you, instead of against you? Creating positive, empowering habits can turn your life around.

How to Build Positive Habits

1.Start Small

Don't try to change everything at once. Pick one habit you want to build, and start small. Want to get fit? Start with a 10-minute workout.

2.Make It Consistent

Consistency is key. Even on days when you don't feel like it, do your habit for just a few minutes. It's better than skipping it altogether.

3.Track Your Progress

Write down your progress or use an app to track your habits. This will keep you motivated and remind you of how far you've come.

Top 25 Motivating Quotes

1."The only limit to our realization of tomorrow is our doubts of today." — Franklin D. Roosevelt

2."Success is not final, failure is not fatal: It is the courage to continue that counts." — Winston Churchill

3."You miss 100% of the shots you don't take." — Wayne Gretzky

4."The harder you work for something, the greater you'll feel when you achieve it."—anonymous

5."Believe in yourself and all that you are. Know that there is something inside you that is greater than any obstacle." — Christian D. Larson

6."Do something today that your future self will thank you for."—Sean Patrick Flanery

7."It always seems impossible until it's done." — Nelson Mandela

8."Don't wait. The time will never be just right." — Napoleon Hill

9."The best way to predict the future is to create it." — Abraham Lincoln

10. "Dream big. Start small. Act now." — Robin Sharma

11. "Success is not how high you have climbed, but how you make a positive difference to the world." — Roy T. Bennett

12. "The only way to do great work is to love what you do." — Steve Jobs

13. "Do not wait for leaders; do it alone, person to person." — Mother Teresa

14. "Great things are not done by impulse, but by a series of small things brought together." — Vincent Van Gogh

15. "The journey of a thousand miles begins with one step." — Lao Tzu

16. "Don't watch the clock; do what it does. Keep going." — Sam Levenson

17. "It's not whether you get knocked down, it's whether you get up." — Vince Lombardi

18. "Act as if what you do makes a difference. It does." — William James

19. "Life is 10% what happens to us and 90% how we react to it." — Charles R. Swindoll

20.“Believe you can and you’re halfway
there.” — Theodore Roosevelt

21.“You are never too old to set another goal or to dream a
new dream.” — C.S. Lewis

22.“Opportunities don’t happen,
you create them.” — Chris Grosser

23.“The way to get started is to quit talking and
begin doing.” — Walt Disney

24.“Don’t be pushed around by the fears in your mind. Be
led by the dreams in your heart.” — Roy T. Bennett

25.“Our greatest glory is not in never falling, but in rising
every time we fall.” — Confucius

These 25 quotes are curated to inspire you, challenge you,
and remind you that no matter the situation, you have the
power within you to keep pushing forward and achieve
great things! Keep these quotes handy for those moments
when you need that extra push or a burst of motivation.

A NOTE TO MYSELF

Acknowledgments

This book is as much a reflection of my journey as it is a collective effort, and I owe a deep gratitude to the people who have been a part of it. First and foremost, to my family—your unconditional love and support have been my guiding light. Through every moment of doubt, confusion, and struggle, you've been the steady hand that helped me back on track. The strength you've given me, often without even realizing it, has been the foundation on which this book was built. I could never have achieved what I have without you.

To my friends and mentors, thank you for your belief in me, for sharing your wisdom, and for challenging me when I needed it most. Your encouragement has fueled my growth and helped me push beyond the limits I once thought I had.

And lastly, to myself, thank you for not giving up. Thank you for turning pain into purpose and using every empty moment to rediscover your strength. This book is as much for you as it is for anyone reading it. And to you, the reader, thank you for joining me on this journey. May you find the strength in your own silence and the courage to transform your own emptiness into something beautiful.